The Story of a Special Day
Volume 33

February

2

The 33rd day of the year. There are 332 days (333 in leap years) remaining until the end of the year.

by Michael Dobson

Timespinner
Press

This book is also available in e-book form for Kindle, e-pub devices, and other formats from your favorite online booksellers.

For more information about the series, about us, or about your special day, please email us at editor@timespinnerpress.com.

Look for other volumes in *The Story of a Special Day*, coming often. See www.timespinnerpress.com for details and for the most recent information.

Table of Contents

Grand Central Station Opens 7

What Happened on February 2? 17

Notable February 2 People 23

Who Was Born on February 2? 25

Who Died on February 2? 37

Holidays Around the World 47

February: The Second Month 61

February in Other Cultures 64

February Symbols 69

February 2 Zodiac Signs 73

What Day of the Week is February 2? 77

On Names and Dates 78

Copyright, Credit, and Contact 83

Other Books from Timespinner Press 91

Cover: Grand Central Terminal, New York. (Photo: Eric Baetscher, CC BY-SA 3.0.) Grand Central Termianl opened at midnight, February 2, 1913 — the EVENT OF THE DAY.

Quote of the Day

"History teaches us that men and nations behave wisely once they have exhausted all other alternatives."

Abba Eban, diplomat and author
born February 2, 1915

Today in History

February 2

Grand Central Station in 1902

Event of the Day
Grand Central Station Opens

At exactly midnight on February 2, 1913, the first train departed from New York City's Grand Central Station. One of the most iconic buildings in New York City, as well as one of the world's most visited tourist attractions, Grand Central has more railroad platforms (44) than any other station in the world. At its height in 1947, 65 million people (over 40% of the entire population of the US) traveled through the facility. It was declared a National Historic Landmark in 1976.

A Brief History of Grand Central

The first building on the site of today's Grand Central was called the Grand Central Depot, where three different railroads came together. It opened October 1871. The growing role of railways in American life soon overwhelmed the original facility, and between 1899 and 1900 it was extensively renovated and expanded, and renamed Grand Central Station.

As steam trains gave way to electric ones, the New York Central Railroad's chief engineer, William Wilgus, wrote a letter to the company president urging that the entire building be torn down and completely replaced so it could better serve the new technology and handle the ever-increasing traffic load.

To pay for the new building, Wilgus pointed out that there was a 16-block open area behind the station, where the tracks ran. He proposed using the space to create a mammoth 12-story, 2.3 million square foot buiilding that would generate enough rent to offset the cost. The company agreed, and Wilgus was picked to head the project.

While there were strong business reasons to favor the project, there was also competition with the Pennsylvania Railroad, which was building its own facility, Pennsylvania Station. Grand Central had to be bigger, better, and more lavish. Two architectural firms collaborated on its design.

The existing facility was torn down and rebuilt in phases. While this doubled costs, it allowed the railroad to continue train service during the ten year construction process.

The project involved 10,000 workers, nearly 120 thousand tons of steel, 33 miles of track, and a total of $43 million (over $1 billion in 2016 dollars).

As previously noted, the new Grand Central opened at midnight on February 2, 1913, with the departure of its first train. A minute later, the first incoming train arrived. Within sixteen hours of its opening, there were over 150,000 visitors.

Architecture

Grand Central was designed using Beaux-Arts style, which used sculptural decoration along with more modern lines. It was built with expansion in mind; the roof could support a future skyscraper.

Construction of the new station

The building's Main Concourse, a long hall with a ceiling 125 feet (38 meters) high, is one of the moust famous and dramatic architectural elements. Outside the station, the 13 foot (4 meter) clock contains the world's largest piece of Tiffany glass, along with the largest sculptural group in the world.

The ceiling of the Main Concourse is painted with an astronomical design. If you look closely, you can see a small dark circle above the constellation Pisces. In 1957, in response to the Soviet Sputnik launch, the US government displayed a Redstone missile inside the Main Concourse. The only way to get it in was to cut a hole in the ceiling, and the dsrk circle is the remaining evidence.

Redstone Missile on display in the Main Concourse (1957)

The Grand Central Zone

The new Grand Central was over twice as large as Penn Station, and contained numerous amenities, including dressing rooms with maid service (at a small fee), and much more.

One level below the Main Concourse is the Dining Concourse, home to the famous Oyster Bar. Numerous restaurants and fast food outlets are available.

It sparked an economic renaissance in the area. Seven luxury hotels, including the Biltmore and the Waldorf Astoria, were built. CBS Television was located in Grand Central from 1939 to 1964, with newscasts and other production taking place in the building.

The Grand Central Art Gallery, the largest sales gallery of art in the world, along with the Grand Central School of Art, occupied space in the building from 1922 to 1958.

Grand Central in Modern Times

As the role of railways declined, Grand Central underwent changes. Donald Trump negotiated tax breaks to build a new Grand Hyatt hotel east of the terminal in exchange for renovating the exterior.

Amtrak stopped service to Grand Central in 1988, and from that time Grand Central only served Metro-North Railroad. At the time of writing, a new access is being built to bring the Long Island Rail

Road into the station as well.

As an iconic image of New York City, Grand Central features in over 40 films, numerous television shows, and even had its own radio anthology program, *Grand Central Station,* which ran from 1937 to 1954.

Secrets of Grand Central

The President's Platform. A special private platform, Track 61, was built primarily for US President Franklin Delano Roosevelt, whose legs were paralyzed from polio. He would travel to the city in his personal train (used by presidents before Air Force One), where he could take a specially designed elevator to the street. The first person to use the special track was actually General John J. Pershing in 1938. It is occasionally used to this day.

The Secret Sub-Basement. In order to power the electric trains, special AC to DC converters are used to supply the traction current to the tracks. They were located in a sub-basement under the terminal known as "M42."

During World War II, it was feared that saboteurs could cripple troop movements in the eastern US with no more than a bucket of sand. In fact, two agents sent by the German Abwehr (military intelligence service) were caught by the FBI in the attempt. Even today, the location of M42 is a closely guarded secret, and the room itself does not appear on any maps of the station.

Radiation. Grand Central Terminal is primarily made of granite. Like many natural stones, granite contains some radioactive isotopes, such as potassium-40, and some granites contain a small amount of uranium. Even though the radiation is high enough to register on a geiger counter, it's still far too low to be a hazard to human health, especially if you're just passing through.

The One-Minute Delay. For safety reasons, every train leaves a minute later than its posted departure time to encourage people to slow down. Even though Grand Central has marble floors, it still has the fewest number of slips and falls of any station in the US.

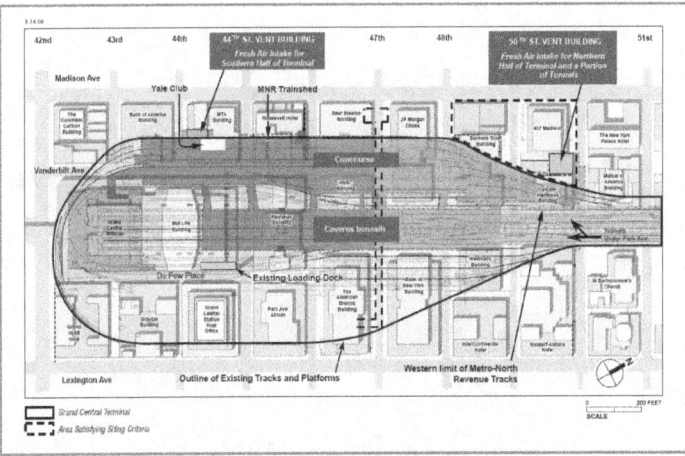

Map of Grand Central Terminal (2006)

Depot. Station. or Terminal?

We've used the popular name "Grand Central Station," but the formal name is actually "Grand Central Terminal." Technically, a *station* (sometimes *depot*)is a place where trains stop to load or unload passengers or freight. A *terminal* (sometimes *terminus*) is a station at the end of a railway line. Grand Central was first a depot, and later a station. It became a terminal in 1988 when Amtrak stopped serving the station, but all it takes is a regular through train before it once again can become Grand Central Station.

All aboard!

Interior detail of Grand Central Station

The famous Oyster Bar

Lead sled dog Balto with musher Gunnar Kaasen, from the last dog team that successfully delivered diphtheria antitoxin to Nome.

What Happened on February 2?

From the creation of great works of engineering and art, to devastating wars and natural disasters, thousands of years of history have left their mark on each and every day of the year. Here are some important events that occurred on February 2. (Illustrated items are boxed.)

1536 — The city of **Buenos Aires**, Argentina, is founded by Spanish *conquistador* Pedro de Mendoza.

1653 — The Dutch settlement of **New Amsterdam** (later **New York**) gains official city status.

1709 — Scottish sailor **Alexander Selkirk**, after four years as a castaway on an uninhabited Pacific island, is rescued. His story is the inspiration for Daniel Defoe's novel *Robinson Crusoe*.

1876 — The first **Groundhog Day in the US** is celebrated.

1901 — The **funeral of Queen Victoria** takes place. *(Photo next page.)*

1922 — James Joyce's novel *Ulysses* is published.

1925 — In the **serum run to Nome**, also known as the Great Race of Mercy, a dog sled relay in Alaska delivers desperately needed supplies of diphtheria antitoxin to the town of Nome, turning lead sled dog Balto into a national canine celebrity and inspiring the annual Iditarod Trail Sled Dog Race.

1943 — After five months of combat and an estimated two million casualties, the World War II **Battle of Stalingrad** ends.

Queen Victoria (Photo: Alexander Bassano)

Civilians in the ruins of Stalingrad (Courtesy German Federal
Archives, CC BY-SA 4.0)

Quote of the Day

"A man of genius makes no mistakes. His errors are volitional and are the portals of discovery."

from *Ulysses,* by James Joyce
born February 2, 1882

Births
and
Deaths

THERM
ACC
MAGNA

February 2

Heavyweight boxing champion John L. Sullivan.
Sullivan died February 2, 1918 (Photo: Jose Maria Mora)

Notable February 2 People

With the current world population at about seven billion people, on average about 19 million people also celebrate their birthdays on February 2 — and that isn't counting the millions and millions who came before! No matter when you were born, you share your birthday with many special people whose accomplishments (and occasionally embarrassments) have been noted as part of history.

In this section, you'll meet fascinating people who share your birthday. They're organized by what they're famous for, and then in reverse chronological order from most recent to earliest. Those who are shown in photographs or artwork have a box around them. We don't have photos of everyone, so please forgive us if your favorite person is missing.

Some of these people you've heard of, others may be new to you, but they all make up an important part of the reason that February 2 is a truly special day!

Solomon R. Guggenheim Museum, New York (Photo: Ad Meskens)

Who Was Born on February 2?

Art and Illustration

Pat Sullivan, cartoonist and animator who produced the *Felix the Cat* silent cartoons. *(1885* — *some sources say 1887)*

Solomon R. Guggenheim, businessman, philanthropist, and modern art collector who built the iconic Guggenheim Museum in New York City. *(1861)*

Business

Dale Mortensen, shared the 2010 Nobel Memorial Prize in Economic Science for his analysis of markets with search frictions. *(1939)*

Howard Johnson, founder of the Howard Johnson hotel and restaurant chain, the first modern restaurant franchise. *(1897)*

Crime and Terrorism

Salem al-Hazmi (سالم الحازمي), one of the hijackers of the plane that crashed into the Pentagon as part of the 9/11 terrorist attacks. *(1981)*

---

* Some sources give 1887 as the year of birth.

Fashion and Modeling

Christie Brinkley, model and actress known for her *Sports Illustrated* swimsuit covers and for having the longest running cosmetics contract of any model in history as the face of CoverGirl for 25 years. *(1954)*

Christie Brinkley (Photo: Martyna Borkowski)

Government and Military

Abba Eban (אבא אבן), Israeli diplomat and politician who served as foreign minister, education minister, deputy prime minister, ambassador to the US, and vice president of the UN General Assembly. *(1915)*

Albert Sidney Johnson, highest ranking officer killed during the American Civil War. *(1803)*

Charles Maurice de Talleyrand-Périgord, influential French diplomat and minister whose power lasted from the regime of Louis XVI through Napoléon and afterward. *(1754[†])*

Charles Maurice de Talleyrand-Périgord

[†] Some sources give February 13 as the day of birth.

Literature and Journalism

Thomas M. Disch, critically acclaimed science fiction and fantasy author whose best known works include the classic *Camp Concentration,* as well as children's books such as *The Brave Little Toaster.* *(1940)*

Judith Viorst, children's author best known for the 1972 book *Alexander and the Terrible, Horrible, No Good, Very Bad Day.* *(1931)*

Walter J. Boyne, Air Force pilot and aviation historian known as the "dean of aviation writers," former director of the Smithsonian Institution's National Air and Space Museum, chairman of the National Aeronautic Association, and co-founder of the cable Wingspan / Air and Space Channel. *(1929)*

Liz Smith, gossip columnist known as the "Grand Dame of Dish." *(1923)*

James Dickey, American poet and novelist best known for his 1970 novel *Deliverance;* served as Poet Laureate of the United States. *(1923)*

Ayn Rand, novelist best known for *The Fountainhead* and *Atlas Shrugged,* created the philosophy known as Objectivism. *(1905‡)*

---

‡ Under the "Old Style" (O.S.) Julian calendar, February 2 is January 20. For an explanation of different calendar dates, see "What Day of the Week is February 2?"

Johnston McCulley, pulp novelist who created Zorro. *(1883)*

James Joyce, Irish novelist and poet considered one of the most influential of the 20th century, author of *Ulysses, Finnegans Wake,* and *Portrait of the Artist as a Young Man. (1882)*

James Joyce (illustration by Djuna Barnes)

Music

Shakira, singer-songwriter whose hits include "Hips Don't Lie." *(1977)*

Graham Nash, singer-songwriter best known as a member of The Hollies and Crosby, Stills, Nash & Young, member of the Rock and Roll Hall of Fame. *(1942)*

Tom Smothers, comedian and musician best known as half of the Smothers Brothers act. *(1937)*

Stan Getz, jazz saxophonist best known for his 1964 bossa nova hit "The Girl from Ipanema." *(1927)*

Burton Lane, composer and lyricist of numerous Broadway musicals, including *Finian's Rainbow* and *On a Clear Day You Can See Forever. (1912)*

Jascha Heifetz, Lithuanian-American violinist considered one of the greatest of all time. *(1901§)*

Performing Arts

Gemma Arterton, English actress best known as a Bond girl role in the 2008 film *Quantum of Solace.* *(1986)*

---

§ Under the "Old Style" (O.S.) Julian calendar, February 2 is January 20. For an explanation of different calendar dates, see "What Day of the Week is February 2?"

The Smothers Brothers (l-r) **Tom Smothers,** Dick Smothers.

Kim Zimmer, actress who won four Daytime Emmys for her roles in the soap operas *Guiding Light* and *One Life to Live. (1955)*

Ina Garten, author, cook, and host of the cooking show *Barefoot Contessa. (1948)*

Farrah Fawcett, actress best known for her role in the TV series *Charlie's Angels,* and for her swimsuit poster that became the best-selling pin-up poster in history. *(1947)*

Farrah Fawcett

David Jason, actor best known to British audiences for his roles in *Only Fools and Horses* and *A Touch of Frost.* *(1940)*

Robert Mandan, actor best known for playing Chester Tate on the 1970s sitcom *Soap.* *(1932)*

Les Dawson, comedian and writer best known to English audiences for his eponymous television show and numerous other appearances. *(1931)*

Elaine Stritch, actress and singer primarily known for her work on Broadway, played the mother of executive Jack Donaghy on the sitcom *30 Rock,* member of the American Theater Hall of Fame. *(1925)*

Nell Gwyn, one of the most famous actresses of the Restoration period in England and long-time mistress of King Charles II, with whom she had two sons. *(1650)* *(Photo next page.)*

Science

Mary-Dell Chilton, chemist who help found the field of modern plant biotechnoloogy, winner of the World Food Prize and member of the National Inventors Hall of Fame. *(1939)*

Nell Gwynn, by Simon Pietersz (Courtesy National Portrait Gallery)

Sports

Donald Driver, wide receiver for the Green Bay
Packers, author of the best-selling memoir *Driven,*
and winner of the 14th season of *Dancing With the
Stars. (1975)*

Doris "Sammye" Sams, outfielder and pitcher in the All-American Girls Professional Baseball League, named player of the year twice. *(1927)*

Red Schoendienst, baseball player, coach, and long-term manager of the St. Louis Cardinals; elected in 1989 to the Baseball Hall of Fame. *(1923)*

1953 Bowman Gum trading card for Red Schoendienst

Wes Ferrell, baseball pitcher whose 37 home runs as a batter remain a career record for an MLB pitcher. *(1908)*

George Halas, football player, coach, and owner of the Chicago Bears, co-founder of the National Football League, one of the original inductees into the Pro Football Hall of Fame. *(1895)*

Natalie Barney

Who Died on February 2?

Government and Military

Chris Kyle, US Navy SEAL who wrote the best-selling autobiography *American Sniper*, which became a 2014 film. (2013)

Hatüey, Caribbean tribal chief who fought the invading Spaniards, considered a Cuban national hero. *(1512)*

Literature and Journalism

Dorothy Gilman, mystery writer best known for the *Mrs. Pollifax* series. (2012)

Claude Brown, best-selling African-American author of the autobiographical 1965 work *Manchild in the Promised Land.* *(2002)*

Alistair MacLean, best-selling author of *The Guns of Navarone, Ice Station Zebra,* and *Where Eagles Dare,* all adapted into films. *(1987)*

Natalie Barney, author of *The Well of Loneliness,* the most famous lesbian novel of the 20th century. *(1972)*

Baldassare Castiglione, Italian courtier and diplomat during the Renaissance period, known for his influential *The Book of the Courtier.* (1529)

Music and Dance

David McComb, singer-songwriter and guitarist for the Australian rock bands The Triffids and The Blackeyed Susans. *(1999)*

Gene Kelly, dancer and actor whose best known films include such Hollywood musicals as *An American in Paris, Singin' in the Rain*, and many others. *(1996)*

Sid Vicious, bass guitarist for the punk band Sex Pistols, allegedly murdered his girlfriend, as told in the 1986 film *Sid and Nancy*. *(1979)*

Performing Arts

Bob Elliott, half of the comedy duo Bob and Ray, father of actor Chris Elliott. *(2016)*

Philip Seymour Hoffman, actor who received an Academy Award for the title role in the 2005 film *Capote*, also known for his portrayal of a CIA officer in *Charlie Wilson's War* and as the villain in *Mission: Impossible III*. *(2014)*

Margaret John, actress best known to British audiences for her role as Doris O'Neil in *Gavin & Stacey*. *(2011)*

Barry Morse, actor best known for his role as Lt. Philip Gerard on the 1960s television series *The Fugitive*. *(2008)*

(l-r) Mitzi Gaynor, Taina Elg, Kay Kendall, and **Gene Kelly** from the 1957 film *Les Girls*

Donald Pleasence, English actor whose best-known roles include Blofeld in the1967 Bond film *You Only Live Twice,* and Lieutenant Blythe in *The Great Escape. (1995)*

Bert Parks, actor and singer best known for hosting the Miss America pageant for more than twenty years. *(1992)*

Boris Karloff, actor best known for his roles in numerous horror films, especially the 1931 version of *Frankenstein. (1969)*

Charlie Grapewin, vaudeville performer and actor who played Uncle Henry in the 1939 film *The Wizard of Oz* and Grandpa Joad in the 1940 film *The Grapes of Wrath. (1956)*

Science and Technology

William Howard Stein, shared the 1972 Nobel Prize in Chemistry for his work on ribonuclease. *(1980)*

Bertrand Russell, British polymath and co-author of *Principia Mathematica,* awarded the1950 Nobel Prize in Literature. *(1970)*

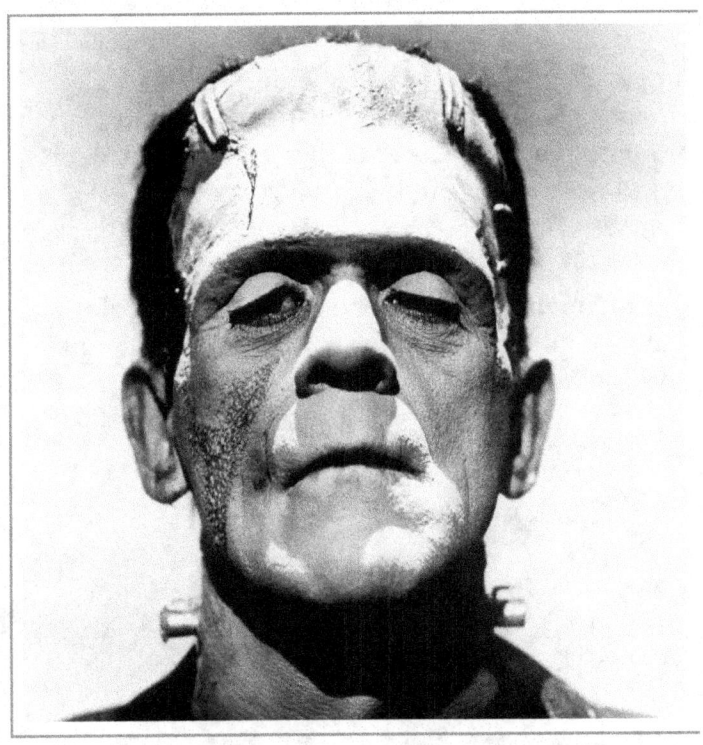

Boris Karloff as the Monster in *Bride of Frankenstein* (1935)

Dmitri Mendeleev (Дми́трий Менделе́ев),
Russian chemist and inventor whose formulation of
the Periodic Law led to the development of the
Periodic Table of Elements. *(1907[**])*

Sports

Pepper Paire, catcher and infielder with the All-
American Girls Professional Baseball League, co-
authored the official league theme song, "Victory
Song," featured in the 1992 film *A League of Their
Own. (2013)*

Max Schmeling, German boxer who was world
heavyweight champion from 1930 to 1932, famous
worldwide for his two fights with Joe Louis. *(2005)*

Max Schmeling (Photo: William C. Green, NYWTS)

[**] Under the "Old Style" (O.S.) Julian calendar, January 20. For an
explanation of different calendar dates, see "What Day of the Week
is February 2?"

Fred Perry, English tennis and table tennis player, first to win a "Career Grand Slam" of all four singles titles. *(1995)*

Truxton Hare, football player and Olympic track and field athlete, charter member of the College Football Hall of Fame. *(1956)*

John L. Sullivan, American boxer recognized as the first heavyweight champion of gloved boxing and the last heavyweight champion of bare-knuckle boxing. *(1918) (Photo page 22.)*

Quote of the Day

"Well, it's Groundhog Day...again."

Bill Murray as "Phil"
from the film *Groundhog Day*.
Groundhog Day is celebrated on February 2.

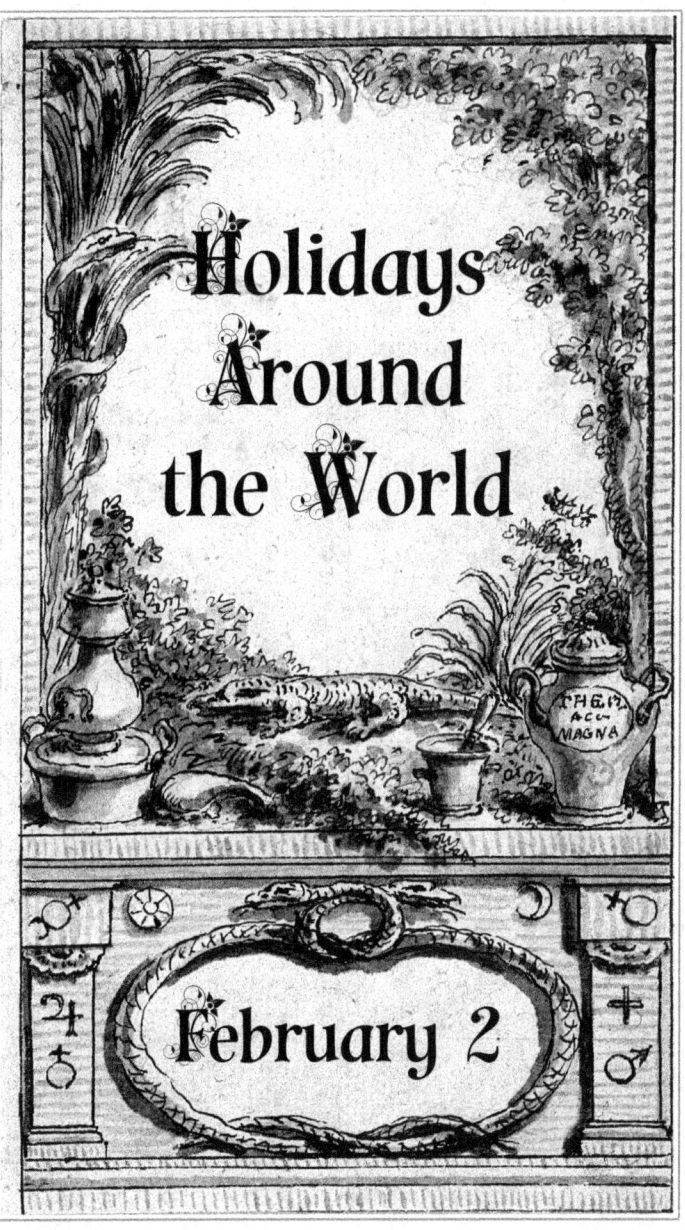

Holidays
Around
the World

CHEM
A C-
MAGNA

February 2

The 2005 Groundhog Day celebration in Punxsutawney,
Pennsylvania (Photo: Aaron Silvers)

Holidays Around the World

If you're looking for a reason to take your special day off, you should know that every single day is a holiday somewhere in the world! Here's some of what you can celebrate on February 2!

Groundhog Day

On Groundhog Day, according to folklore, if it is cloudy when a groundhog emerges from its burrow on February 2, then spring will arrive early. If it's sunny, the groundhog will supposedly see its shadow and retreat back into its den, extending winter weather for six more weeks.

Groundhog Day originated in the German community of southeastern Pennsylvania (known colloquially as the Pennsylvania Dutch, a corruption of *Deutch,* or German). It comes from European weather legends in which a badger or bear, rather than a groundhog, does the predicting. Some sources claim that Groundhog Day is related to the pagan festival of Imbolc, celebrated on February 1, because Imbolc also involved predictions about the weather.

In America, the first mention of Groundhog Day dates back to 1841, but only became widespread in 1887 when the town of Punxutawney, Pennsylvania, began an annual Groundhog Day festival, made famous in the 1993 film *Groundhog Day.* Today, other towns in Pennsylvania, Ontario, Nova Scotia, and Texas have their own festivals.

Smaller celebrations take place in Groundhog Lodges, where the Pennsylvania German dialect is the only one spoken. Anyone who speaks English has to pay a small penalty.

Groundhogs aren't the only animals who predict the weather. In Alaska, **Marmot Day** is celebrated instead. Nevada has a similar tradition using a desert tortoise named **Mojave Max**. In Shreveport, Louisiana, **Claude the Cajun Crawfish** does the prediction.

General Events

Anniversary of the Treaty of Tartu (*Tartu rahulepingu aastapäev***)** in Estonia celebrates the treaty that ended the Estonian War of Independence.

Constitution Day (*Araw ng Saligang Batas***)** in the Philippines celebrates the ratification of the 1987 Constitution in that country.

Day of Youth (Azerbaijan) honors youth in that country.

Inventor's Day (*Wan Nak Pradit***)** in Thailand commemorates the patent for a paddle wheel aereator invented by King Bhuimbol.

On **Liichtmëssdag,** in Luxembourg, children go door to door holding lanterns and singing traditional songs, for which they receive a small reward, such as sweets or coins.

Nickanan Night in Cornwall, UK, also known as Roguery Night, is a day of mischief, similar to Halloween.

World Wetlands Day commemorates the Ramsar Convention for conserving wetlands, which was signed February 2, 1971.

Celebrations About Food

In the United States, almost every day of the year is dedicated to a particular food. (Some other countries also have official food days, but only in America is there one every single day!) Sponsored by manufacturers, retailers, farmers, or simply fans, these days are often proclaimed by the President, Congress, state governors, or mayors. Given that there are more different foods than days of the year, some days honor more than one kind of food!

Some foods just get a day, while others get a whole month. Here's what to eat on February 2 and the rest of the month of February!

Food Days

National Tater Tot Day. Tater Tots is a trademark of Ore-Ida for a dish made of deep-fried grated potatoes, though the term is used for similar products.

If February 2 is the first Saturday of the month, it's also **Ice Cream for Breakfast Day**.

In France, the celebration of **Candlemas** (see "Religious Feast Days and Holidays") is also known as **Le Jour des Crêpes**, or The Day of the Crêpes. If you can catch the crêpe with a frying pan after tossing it into the air with your right hand while holding a gold coin in your left hand, you will become rich that year.

Honorary Food Months

- Canned Food Month
- National Chocolate Lovers Month
- National Cherry Month
- National Grapefruit Month
- National Hot Breakfast Month
- National Snack Food Month
- National Potato Lovers Month

- Return Shopping Carts to the Supermarket Month

An abandoned shopping cart, by Michiel1972 (CC BY-SA 3.0) for RETURN SHOPPING CARTS TO THE SUPERMARKET MONTH

Religious Feast Days and Holidays

Every religion normally has feast days and holidays associated with it. While some religious days take place on a given calendar day, others occur on different days each year, usually because the date is determined by the phases of the Moon rather than the Earth's path around the Sun. Here are some religious feasts, festivals, and holidays that sometimes or always fall on February 2!

Candlemas (Western Christianity)

The Christian holiday of Candlemas, formally known as the Feast of the Presentation of Jesus at the Temple, takes place on the 40th day after Chrismas. In the Philippines, the holiday is known as Our Lady of the Candles; in Tenerife, and it's the celebrationof the Virgin of Candelaria. In many cultures, pancakes or a related food are eaten: in France, crêpes; in Mexico, tamales.

Celebration of Yemanjá (Candomblé)

In the Candomblé religion, practiced mainly in Brazil, the feast of the pagan goddess Yemanjá (Queen of the Ocean) is celebrated on February 2.

Shrove Monday

Shrove Monday, the Monday prior to Ash Wednesday, which begins the season of Lent, is celebrated 46 days prior to Easter Sunday. Because the date of Easter is based on the lunar cycle, Shrove Monday takes place on different days each year, as early as February 2 or as late as March 8.

The word "shrove" describes the practice of seeking absolution for sins and doing penance as part of the Lenten observance, so Shrove Monday is often observed with religious services.

However, there are secular observances as well.

The British call it Collop Monday, for a traditional dish of leftover meat and eggs. In Cornwall, pea soup is more common, so it's called Peasen Monday. The Germans call it *Rosenmontag* (Rose Monday). In Iceland, it's *Bolludagur* (Bun Day), and in Denmark it's *Fastelavn.*

Shrove Tuesday (Mardi Gras)

The religious observance of Shrove Tuesday is similar to that of Shrove Monday, but Shrove Tuesday is better known for its secular version, Mardi Gras (French for "Fat Tuesday"). The New Orleans Mardi Gras celebration is perhaps the most famous, but Mardi Gras and the Carnival season (between Ephiphany and Ash Wednesday) are celebrated in many areas with large Catholic populations. It's known as *Karneval* or *Fasching* in Germany, *Martedi Grasso* in Italy, and *Fettisdagen* in Sweden.

While Mardi Gras is always on a Tuesday, many Caribbean nations celebrate their Carnival on Lundi Gras ("Fat Monday") instead.

Mardi Gras can take place anywhere from February 3 to March 9 in regular years, and from February 2 to March 9 in leap years.

Sheet music for the "Mardi Gras Rag," 1914

Saint Days

Each day in the year is considered a feast day for one or more saints. They are somewhat different in western Christianity (Catholicism and many forms of Protestantism) and in eastern (Orthodox) Christianity. The list of saints, martyrs, and others is quite extensive, so not all are necessarily listed.

In **Western Christianity,** February 2 is the feast day of Cornelius the Centurion.

In **Eastern Orthodox Christianity,** it is also the commemoration of Saints Apronian, Flosculu, Laurence of Canterbury, Adalbald, Feock, Hadeloga, Marquard, Theodoric, and Columbanus. (These saints are honored on January 20 by "Old Calendrists.")

Honorary Months

Presidents, Congresses, and nations around the world issue proclamations recognizing particular months to honor certain causes. These events generally fall in February, though honorary months do come and go. Holidays established by states and nonprofit organizations are listed if verified. If not otherwise specified, all months are US. There is some variation from year to year; some celebratory months get added and others get dropped. Two places to get up to date information are the current edition of *Chase's Calendar of Events* or the website Brownielocks. Here are some honorary designations for February.

Black History Month (United States, Canada)
One of the most famous honorary months is Black History Month (sometimes African-American History Month). During Black History Month, important people and events in the African diaspora are commemorated. In the US and Canada, Black History Month is observed in February; in the UK, it's October.

"The First Vote," by Alfred Waud (1867)

Other honorary month designations for February include:

- American Heart Month
- Grapefruit Month
- International Month of Black Women in the Arts
- International Prenatal Infection Prevention Month
- LGBT History Month (United Kingdom)
- Library Lovers Month
- Marijuana Awareness Month
- National Bird-Feeding Month
- National Cherry Month
- National Condom Month
- National Children's Dental Health Month
- National Haiku Writing Month
- Pet Dental Health Month
- Season for Nonviolence (January 30-April 4, worldwide)
- Spunky Old Broads Month
- Youth Leadership Month

Moveable and Multi-Day Events

Some events take place over a specific week or time period. Start and finish dates may vary from year to year. Some events occur on different days each year (such as "fourth Saturday of a month"). These events sometimes take place on February 2.

First Week (begins January 29-February 4)

- Doppleganger Week (change your profile picture to someone else)
- Snow Sculpting Week (US)
- Women's Heart Week
- World Interfaith Harmony Week
- Children's Authors and Illustrators Week (first full week)

First Saturday (February 1-7)

- Take Your Child to the Library Day

First Sunday (February 1-7)

- Mother's Day (Kosovo)
- Super Bowl Sunday (US)

Just for Fun

Anybody can make up a holiday, and many people do! While none of these are officially recognized and some may come and go, here are a few more holidays for February 2.

- Ayn Rand Day
- Hedgehog Day
- Play Your Ukulele Day
- Sled Dog Day

Quote of the Day

"The most serious charge which can be brought against New England is not Puritanism but February."

Joseph Wood Krutch, critic,
in *The Twelve Seasons* (1949)

About the Month of February

"February," from the *Brevarium Grimani* by Simon Bening (c.1510)

February: The Second Month

The February sunshine steeps your boughs
And tints the buds and swells the leaves within.

— *William Cullen Bryant, "Among the Trees"*

The month of February takes its name from the Latin word *februum*, meaning purification, because the traditional Roman festival Februa, involving ritual purification, took place in what we now know as mid-February each year.

Because the Romans considered winter to be a monthless period, neither January nor February existed in the Roman calendar until 713 BCE, and when February did become a month, it was the last month of the year!

The number of days in February also varied in ancient times because the calendar had to be periodically adjusted to stay in line with the seasons. In some years, it was only 23 days long. When the calendar and the seasons got too far out of alignment, the Romans added a bonus month, called Intercalaris, consisting of 27 days, to bring everything back on track.

Our modern month of February begins with the calendar reforms of Julius Caesar, known as the Julian[††] calendar. February became 28 days long, with an extra "leap day" added every four years.

———————————

[††] For an explanation of calendar types, see "What Day of the Week is February 4?"

Although the Julian calendar remained stable for a long time, it wasn't perfectly accurate, and the calendar gradually drifted away from the seasons again.

In 1582, under Pope Gregory XIII, the Julian calendar gave way to the Gregorian calendar, still in use today. One of the Gregorian reforms was to eliminate Leap Year when a new century was not divisible by four. As a result, 1800 and 1900 were leap years, but 2000 was not.

Although the pronunciation "feb-roo-err-ee" is preferred, the common pronunciation "feb-ew-err-ee" (as if the month was spelled "Feb-u-ary") is acceptable as well.

From the point of view of meteorologists, February is the third month of winter in the northern hemisphere and the third month of summer in the southern hemisphere.

February always starts on the same day of the week as March and November in common years, and on the same day as August in leap years. It ends on the same weekday as October in all years, and in common years also ends on the same weekday as January. In leap years, February is the only month that ends on the same day of the week as it began.

Because February is the only month with 28 days in common years, it is the only month that can pass without a single full moon. This happened in 1999 and will happen again in 2018. It is also the only month (in common years) that can have exactly four full 7-day weeks. This happens once every six years and twice every eleven years.

"February," by Joachim von Sandrart

February in Other Cultures

The month of February has different names in different languages. Some nations use calendars other than the Gregorian, and their months may overlap with February. In lunar-based calendars, such as the Islamic calendar, months move through the seasons. Still, many languages often have a word for February itself.

Albanian: Shkurt

Anglo-Saxon: Sol-monath (cake month)

Arabic (Egypt, Sudan, Yemen): يونأغينافبراير (fibrāyir)

Arabic (Levant): حزيركانوشباط (shubāṭ)

Arabic (Libya): الصهناالنوار (an-nuwwār)

Arabic (Algeria and Tunisia): جأيفيفري (Fīfrī)

Arabic (Morocco): غينافبراير (fibrāyər)

Azerbaijani: Fevral

Basque: Otsail

Bulgarian: февруари (fevruari)

Chinese: 二月 (Cantonese: yihyuht; Mandarin: èryuè; Taiwanese: ji-goeh)

Corsican: Ferraghju

Croatian: Veljačaj

Czech: únor (month of submerging)

Finnish: Helmikuu (month of the pearl)

French: Février

German/Danish/Norwegian/Slovenian: Februar

Greek: Φεβρουάριος (Febrouários)

Haitian Creole: Fevriye

Hebrew: ינפברואר (febru'ar)

Hindi: फ़रवरी (farvarī)

Hungarian: Február

Irish (Gaelic): Feabhra mí Feabhra

Italian: Febbraio

Japanese (traditional calendar): 二月 (nigatsu); 如月(kisaragi)

Kazakh: Ақпан (Aḳpan)

Korean: 이월 (iweol)

Lithuanian: Vasaris

Maori: Hui tanguru

Old English: Solmōnaþ (mud month); Kale-monath (cabbage month)

Polish: Luty (month of ice)

Portuguese: Fevereiro

Russian: февраль (fevrali)

Scottish Gaelic: an Gearran

Sesotho: Hlakola

Spanish: Febrero

Swahili/Dutch/Swedish: Februari

Swazi: iNdlovana

Thai: Kumphaphan

Turkish: şubat

Ukrainian: лютий (ljutyj) (month of hard frost)

Vietnamese: 腩㐌 (tháng ha)

Walloon: Fevrî

Welsh: Chwefror

Yiddish: פֿעברואַר (februar)

Zulu: uFebruwari

February Sayings and Superstitions

Here are some sayings and superstitions associated with the month of February.

February Weather Superstitions

February 12 to 14 were said to be "borrowed" from January. If those days were stormy, the year would have good weather, but if they were clear, the rest of the year would be foul.

When the cat lies in the sun in February / She will creep behind the stove in March.

Of all the months of the year / Curse a fair February.

If it thunders in February, it will frost in April.

If February give much snow / A fine summer it doth foreshow

February Wedding Superstitions

A February bride will be an affectionate wife / And a tender mother.

Married in February's sleepy weather / Life you'll tread in time together.

When February birds do mate / You wed nor dread your fate.

In Morocco, there is a ban on marriage during the seven days of *hesoum* (February 24 to March 4)

Valentine's Day Superstitions

The first man an unmarried woman sees on February 14 will be her future husband.

On Valentine's Day, if a girl writes all the names of her suitors on paper, wraps them in clay, and puts them in water, the piece that rises to the top first is the name of her husband to be.

If a woman sees a robin flying overhead on Valentine's Day, she will marry a sailor. If she sees a sparrow, she will marry a poor man but be very happy. If she sees a goldfinch, she will marry a rich person (happiness not guaranteed).

Leap Year Superstitions

Traditionally, women can propose to men on leap days, because the day had no legal status and therefor traditions did not apply. At one time, there was a Scottish law forbidding a man to refuse such a proposal. To ensure success, women should wear a red petticoat under their dress— and make sure it's partially visible to the man when they propose.

In some European countries, if a man refuses a woman's proposal on February 29, he must buy her 12 pairs of gloves.

In Scotland, it's considered unlucky to be born on a Leap Year's Day. Greeks consider it unlucky to be married during a leap year, and especially on a leap day. If you divorce during a leap year, you will never find happiness again.

February Symbols

Birthstone: Amethyst, representing piety, humility, spiritual wisdom, and sincerity

Birth Flowers: Violet and Primrose

Soviet postage stamp of an amethyst from the 1963 "Precious Stone of the Urals" series

Violet (Photo: Andrew Bossi CC BY-SA 2.5)

Still life (primroses, pears, and pomegranates),
by Henri Fantin-Latour

"February," by Eugène Grasset

Michael Dobson

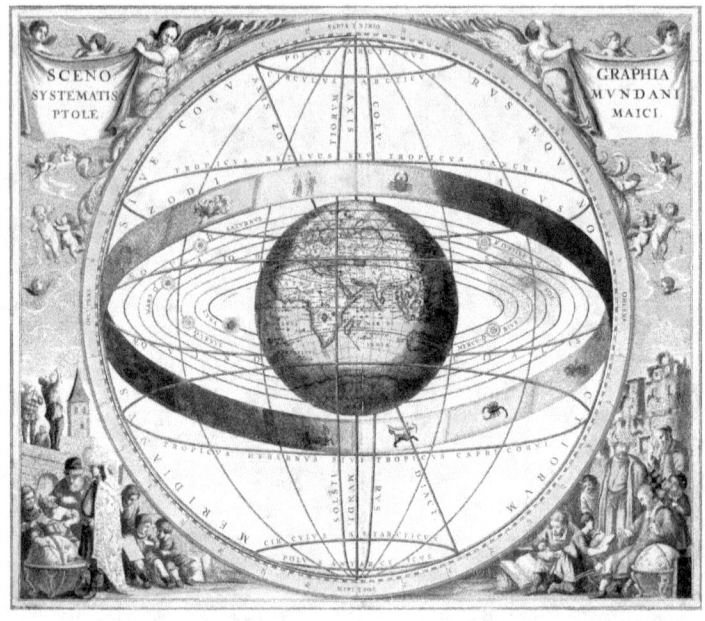

Scenography of the Ptolemaic Cosmography, by Johannes van Loon, based on Andreas Cellarius's *Harmonia Macrocosmica,* 1660

February 2 Zodiac Signs

From the perspective of someone on Earth, the Sun appears to move through the sky throughout the year, along a path astronomers call the *ecliptic plane*. The ecliptic plane is divided into twelve constellations, known as the zodiac, based on traditionally observed patterns of stars. On your birthday, you can't see your constellation, because it's in the daytime sky.

The zodiac was first developed by Babylonian astronomers about 2,500 years ago. Because they were unaware that the Earth wobbles like a spinning top (known as *precession*), they didn't make allowance for the fact that the Sun's path through the zodiac changes over time.

That means there are now two sets of dates for your birth sign. The *tropical dates* are the original Babylonian dates; the *sidereal dates* tell you where the Sun actually appears as it moves along its annual path.

For February 2, the tropical sign is **Aquarius** and the sidereal sign is **Capricorn.**

Aquarius

Tropical January 20 to February 19
Sidereal February 12 to March 8 (March 9 in leap years)

Aquarius is one of the oldest recognized constellations, originally representing the Babylonian god Ea. In Latin, Aquarius means "water-carrier," represented in its symbol. In Greek mythology, Aquarius is sometimes associated with Deucalion, who survived a world-cleansing flood. In Chinese astronomy, it is known as the Black Tortoise of the North (北方玄武, Běi Fāng Xuán Wǔ).

In astrology, Aquarius is considered to be masculine and extroverted, and despite the name is an air sign. Aquarians are supposed to be philanthropical, inventive, and individualistic.

Capricorn

Tropical December 22 to January 20
Sidereal January 15 to February 14

The origins of the constellation Capricorn date back
to Sumeria and Babylonia. Based on Enki, the
Sumerian god of wisdom and waters, Capricorn has
the head and upper body of a mountain goat and the
lower body and tail of a fish. The mountain goat
represents ambition and intelligence, the fish
represents passion and spirituality.

An earth sign, Capricorn is ruled by the planet
Saturn. They are often thought to be responsible,
patient, ambitious and loyal, but can sometimes be
seen as conceited, distrusting, and unimaginative.
Capricornians are supposed to be compatible with
Taurus, Pisces, and Virgo, but not with Aries,
Sagittarius, or Leo.

Illustration by Edward Penfield

What Day of the Week is February 2?

On what day of the week does February 2 fall?

Surprisingly, this isn't an easy question. Because the calendar year is 365 days long (366 in leap years), it doesn't divide evenly by the seven days of the week.

Also, the Earth goes around the Sun in about 365-1/4 days, so a calendar tends to drift over time. That's why the same date falls on different weekdays in different years.

This is made even more complicated by a change in calendars that took place in 1582. Our modern calendar has its roots in ancient Rome, in a calendar reform conducted by Julius Caesar. Caesar commissioned mathematicians to attack the problem, and they came up with the idea of leap years, and thus standardized the calendar for centuries to come. This was called the Julian calendar.

Over time, however, the small errors in Caesar's calculation compounded. That's why Pope Gregory XIII commissioned the Gregorian calendar, used in most of the world today. Some countries converted in 1582, when the calendar was first developed; some converted later; other still haven't changed.

Gregorian and Julian aren't the only types of calendars. The Hebrew year, the Islamic year, and many other calendars are used in different parts of the world and among different people.

You can convert Gregorian dates to other calendars, including the Hebrew calendar, the Islamic calendar, and even the Mayan calendar by visiting the Fourmilab Calendar Converter at http://www.fourmilab.ch/documents/calendar/.

Chinese calendar systems are quite complex and have changed several times; a full discussion is far beyond the scope of this book. If you're interested, you can find information here: http://www.hermetic.ch/cal_stud/chinese_cal.htm.

On Names and Dates

Historians use "CE" (Common Era) and "BCE" (Before the Common Era) instead of the more common "AD" (Anno Domini, or Year of Our Lord) and "BC" (Before Christ), reflecting the fact that the year-numbering system established by the Gregorian calendar is used throughout the world in many countries not culturally Christian.

The CE/BCE designation dates back to at least 1708, and has been adopted as a standard by the United Nations and the Universal Postal Union. Because this series of books covers events and people of all nations and cultures, we use the CE/BCE terms.

The abbreviation "O.S." ("Old Style") and "N.S." ("New Style") on some dates refers to the fact that the Russian Empire (in particular) did not switch from the Julian to the Gregorian calendar at the same time as the rest of Europe, and therefore some figures and events have two dates.

Also, in the Julian calendar in England in the 16th century, the year began on March 25 rather than January 1. To avoid confusion with Gregorian dates, dates between January and March were often written using both years.

People and events whose original names are not in the Western alphabet have their native names (where possible) in the appropriate script shown in parenthesis. If you are using an e-reader to access an electronic version of this book, all characters don't always display on all devices.

A 50-year brass perpetual calendar.

Quote of the Day

"Time is an illusion, lunchtime doubly so."

Douglas Adams,
from *The Hitchhiker's Guide to the Galaxy*

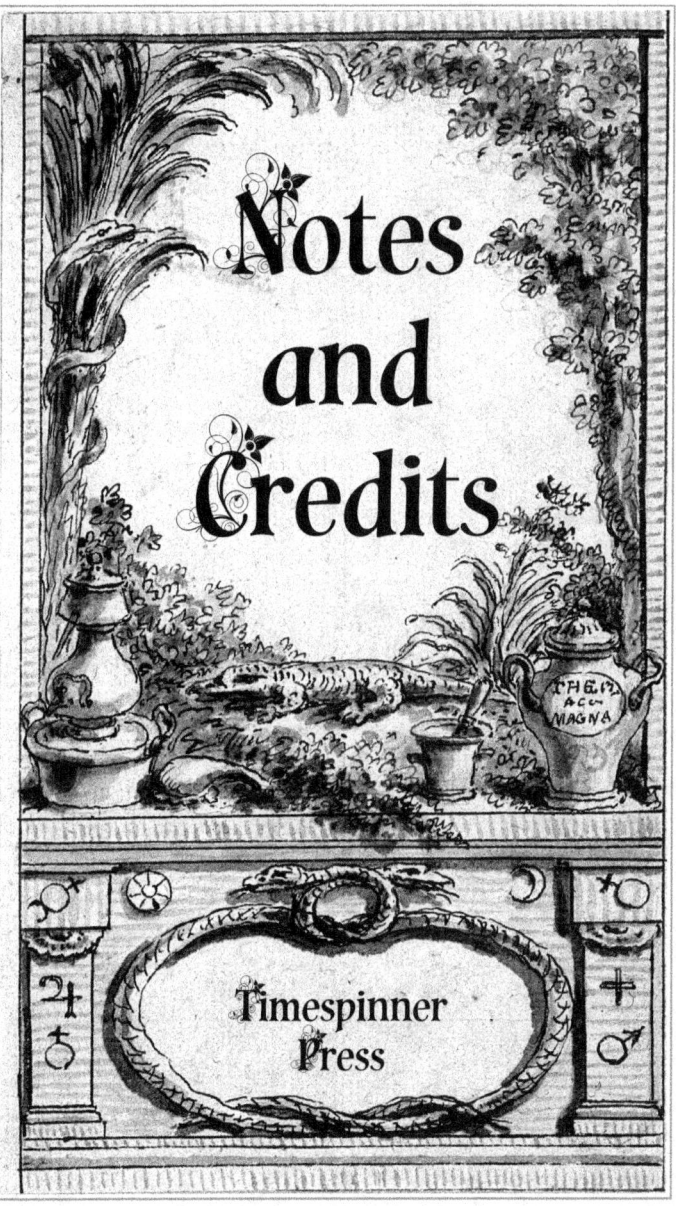

Notes and Credits

Timespinner
Press

Cartoon by John T. McCutcheon

Copyright, Credit, and Contact

Follow Us

Our blog "This Day in History" (http://
timespinnerpress.com/this-day-in-history/) features short
articles on events and people associated with each day, and
updates several times each week. Also subscribe to the
"Quote of the Day" at http://timespinnerpress.com/quote-
of-the-day/. You can get daily links by following us on
Facebook at TimespinnerPress, or on Twitter as
@sidewisethinker.

Contact Us

Find an error or a format problem? Want information about
the series, about us, or about when the volume for your
special day might be available? Please email us at
editor@timespinnerpress.com. (We also take requests if your
special day isn't yet complete. Please give us at least six
weeks' notice if possible.)

Sources

We owe a great debt to Wikipedia, which is our first stop for
research. We attempt to make independent confirmation of
all important dates and facts through a variety of other
sources.

Other sources we frequently use include the Library of
Congress; "on this day" listings from *Encyclopedia Britannica*,
the *New York Times*, and the BBC; Omniglot for the names of
months in other languages; *Chase's Calendar of Events*; and, of
course, the always essential Google.

All art and photographs are either in the public domain, used under a Creative Commons license, or with a "fair use" justification, and most frequently come from Wikimedia Commons and the Library of Congress Prints and Photographs Division.

Attribution is provided where possible, or as requested by the copyright owner, or when there is particular historical significance, listed below. For information about any particular illustration or photograph, please contact us.

Credits

1. The January 2008 photograph of Grand Central Terminal in New York City was taken by Eric Baetscher, and was a Featured Picture on Wikimedia Commons. It is used here under CC BY-SA 3.0.

2. The illustration of the month of February used on the back cover is from the French Gothic illuminated manuscript *Les Très Riches Heures du duc de Berry* by the Limbourg Brothers, Jean Colombe, and an intermediate painter whose name is lost to history. It is in the public domain because its copyright has expired.

3. The box graphic used on the first page is from a 1916 pamphlet entitled "Divorce versus Democracy" authored by G. K. Chesterton, originally published in London by the Society of St. Peter and St. Paul. It is in the public domain in the US because it was published prior to 1923, and is in the public domain in all countries (including the country of origin) in which the copyright time is the author's life plus 70 years or less.

4. The graphic design for the section pages in this book is from a design originally created for a pharmacy label. It is courtesy of Wellcome Images (ICV No 11073, photo V0010813), and is used here under CC BY-SA 4.0.

5. The 1902 postcard of the original Grand Central Station is in the public domain because its copyright has expired. The original artist and publisher are unknown.

6. The photograph of construction on Grand Central Station was taken circa 1908 for the Detroit Publishing Company, and is courtesy Library of Congress (digital ID det.4a22981). It is in the public domain because its copyright has expired.

7. The 1957 photograph of a Redstone missile on display at Grand Central Station is courtesy US Army, and is in the public domain as a work created by an officer or employee of the US government as part of that person's official duties.

8. The 2006 map of Grand Central Terminal is courtesy Federal Transit Administration, and is in the public domain as a work created by an officer or employee of the US government as part of that person's official duties.

9. The photograph of the incline from subway to suburban concourse in Grand Central Station was taken between 1910 and 1920 for the Detroit Publishing Company, and is courtesy Library of Congress (digital ID det.4a24546). It is in the public domain because its copyright has expired.

10. The photograph of the Oyster Bar in Grand Central Station was taken between 1910 and 1920 for the Detroit Publishing Company, and is courtesy Library of Congress (digital ID det.4a24550). It is in the public domain because its copyright has expired.

11. The photograph of sled dog Balto with musher Gunnar Kaasen was taken in 1925 by the Brown Brothers. It is in the public domain because it contains materials that originally came from the National Institutes of Health.

12. The 1887 photograph of Queen Victoria by Alexander Bassano is in the public domain because its copyright has expired.

13. The 1942 photograph of civilians in the ruins of Stalingrad is courtesy German Federal Archives (Bundesarchiv Bild 183-B29644), and is used here under CC BY-SA 4.0.

14. The 1882 photograph of boxer John L. Sullivan was taken by Jose Maria Mora. It is in the public domain because its copyright has expired.

15. The 2012 photograph of the Guggenheim Museum was taken by Ad Meskens, and is used here under CC BY-SA 3.0.

16. The 2008 photograph of Christie Brinkley at the Metropolitan Opera opening is © Rubenstein; the

photograph was taken by Martyna Borkowski. It is used here under CC BY-SA 2.0.

17. The 1850 engraving of Charles-Maurice de Talleyrand is in the public domain because its copyright has expired. It is based on an earlier painting by François Pascal Simon Gérard.

18. The 1922 illustration of James Joyce is by Djuna Barnes, and was originally published in *Vanity Fair*. It is in the public domain because its copyright has expired.

19. The 1965 publicity photograph of The Smothers Brothers is in the public domain because it was published in the United States between 1923 and 1977 without a copyright notice. Traditionally, publicity photographs have not been copyrighted because of the way in which they are intended to be used.

20. The 1965 publicity photograph of Farrah Fawcett is in the public domain because it was published in the United States between 1923 and 1977 without a copyright notice. Traditionally, publicity photographs have not been copyrighted because of the way in which they are intended to be used.

21. The painting of Nell Gwyn is by Simon Pietersz, and dates from about 1680. It is in the public domain because its copyright has expired. The original can be found in the National Portrait Gallery, London.

22. The 1953 Bowman Gum baseball card of Red Schoendienst is in the public domain because it was published in the US between 1923 and 1963. Although there may or may not have been an original copyright notice, the copyright was not renewed and the image is therefore in the public domain.

23. The photograph of Natalie Barney is courtesy Library of Congress (digital ID ggbain.05315). It is in the public domain because its copyright has expired.

24. The 1957 publicity photograph from the film *Les Girls* is in the public domain because it was published in the United States between 1923 and 1977 without a copyright notice. Traditionally, publicity photographs have not been

copyrighted because of the way in which they are intended to be used.

25. The 1957 publicity photograph of Boris Karloff from the 1935 film *Bride of Frankenstein* is in the public domain because it was published in the United States between 1923 and 1977 without a copyright notice. Traditionally, publicity photographs have not been copyrighted because of the way in which they are intended to be used.

26. The 1938 photogrph of Max Schmeling was taken by William C. Green, staff photographer for the New York World-Telegram & Sun (NYWTS). It is from the NYWTS collection donated to the Library of Congress (digital ID cph.3c25851), and per the Instrument of Gift, it is in the public domain.

27. The 2005 Groundhog Day photographis by Aaron Silvers, and is used here under CC BY-SA 2.0.

28. The sheet music cover for the 1914 song "Mardi Gras Rag", by Lyons and Yosco, was published by Geo. W. Meyer Music Co., New York. It is in the public domain because it was first published prior to January 1, 1923.

29. The illustration "The First Vote" by Alfred R. Waud originally appeared on the cover of *Harper's* magazine in 1867. It is in the public domain because its copyright has expired.

30. The painting "February" is from the *Brevarium Grimani*, circa 1510, and is in the public domain because its copyright has expired.

31. The painting "February" by Joachim von Sandrart is in the public domain because its copyright has expired. The original can be found in the Staatsgalerie im Neuen Schloss, Schleißheim, Germany.

32. The 1815 woodcut of a proposal is in the public domain because its copyright has expired.

33. The 1896 drawing "February" by Eugène Grasset is in the public domain because its copyright has expired.

34. The 1963 Soviet postage stamp of an amethyst from the "Precious Stones of the Urals" series is not an object of copyright according to article 1259 of Book IV of the Civil Code of the Russian Federation No. 230-FZ, 12/18/2006.

35. The photograph of violets at the Abbey Church of Saint Peter, Salzburg, Austria, was taken by Andrew Bossi and used here under CC BY-SA 2.5.

36. The painting *"Nature morte (primevères, poires et grenades)"* by Henri Fantin-Latour is in the public domain because its copyright has expired. The original can be found at the Kröller-Müller Museum, Otterlo, Netherlands. Image courtesy Google Art Project by way of Wikimedia Commons.

37. The celestial sphere is from *Scenography of the Ptolemaic Cosmography*, by Johannes van Loon, based on Andreas Cellarius's *Harmonia Macrocosmica*, 1660. It is in the public domain because its copyright has expired.

38. The 1906 automobile calendar is by Edward Penfield, and is in the collection of the Library of Congress Prints and Photographs Division. It is in the public domain because its copyright has expired.

39. The 50-year perpetual calendar photograph is in the public domain.

40. The cartoon by John T. McCutcheon is from his 1905 collection *The Mysterious Stranger and Other Cartoons by John T. McCutcheon.* It is in the public domain because its copyright has expired.

41. The 1866 painting "February in the Isle of Wight" by John Brett is in the public domain because its copyright has expired. The image is courtesy Google Art Project; the original can be found in the Birmingham Museum and Art Gallery.

Timespinner Press

License Description and Terms

Aside from material purely in the public domain, photographs and other material in this book are used under specific licenses permitting free use, usually with an attribution requirement. For full text and terms of these licenses, click or enter the appropriate links below. If you believe there is an error in the copyright status or attribution of any of these images, please email us.

- Creative Commons Attribution 2.0 Generic (CC-BY 2.0): http://creativecommons.org/licenses/by/2.0/deed.en
- Creative Commons Attribution-Share Alike 3.0 Generic (CC-BY-SA 3.0): http://creativecommons.org/licenses/by-sa/3.0/
- Creative Commons Attribution-Share Alike 2.5 Generic (CC-BY-SA 2.5): http://creativecommons.org/licenses/by-sa/2.5/deed.en
- Creative Commons Attribution-Share Alike 2.0 Generic (CC-BY-SA 2.0): http://creativecommons.org/licenses/by/2.0/deed.en
- Creative Commons Attribution-Share Alike 1.0 Generic (CC-BY-SA 1.0): http://creativecommons.org/licenses/by-sa/1.0/deed.en
- CC0 1.0 Universal (CC0 1.0) Public Domain Dedication (CC0 1.0) http://creativecommons.org/publicdomain/zero/1.0/deed.en
- GNU Free Documentation License (GFDL): http://en.wikipedia.org/wiki/Wikipedia:Text_of_the_GNU_Free_Documentation_License
- License Art Libre (Free Art License): http://artlibre.org

"February in the Isle of Wight," John Brett (1866)

Other Books from Timespinner Press

The Story of a Special Day
Michael Dobson

A series of (eventually) 366 volumes covering everything that happened on your special day! Events, births, deaths, quotes, holidays, and much more. It's like a birthday card they'll never throw away!

US$7.95 print/US$2.99 ebook.

From Plassey to Pakistan
Humayun Mirza

The history of British Colonial India and the formation of Pakistan from the unique perspective of the son of Pakistan's first president and last of the royal line of Bengal, Bihar, and Orissa! This unique historical document tells the inside story of this distinguished family, including the detailed story of the coup that toppled his father from power!

US$27.95 print

A Whole New Navy: America's War in the Pacific

Miles Durr

The most comprehensive and detailed description of America's naval war in the Pacific ever—every battle, every ship, every task force and every task group from Pearl Harbor through the Japanese surrender! A must-have for the collection of every World War II buff!

US$29.95 print

Improbable History: The Weird, the Obscure, and the Strangely Important

edited by Michael Dobson

From the birth of Western civilization to the rescue of Apollo 13, from the Leaning Tower of Pisa to Florence's Duomo, history has often turned on small, improbable details. Whatever happened to the ancient Samaritan people? Why did a fortuitous rainstorm allow the British to conquer India? How did an air raid in Italy lead to the development of chemotherapy? What happened when Albert Einstein met Adolf Hitler on the streets of Berlin? How did the Japanese manage to attack the US mainland using balloons? A cast of award-winning writers tackle some of the strangest tales in history!

US$19.95 print

www.ingramcontent.com/pod-product-compliance
Lightning Source LLC
Chambersburg PA
CBHW060153290526
45789CB00003B/1021